BOOK

Written by Vincent Jooris and Marc Sigala
Translated by Ciaran Traynor

Gargantua
BY FRANÇOIS RABELAIS

Bright
≡**Summaries**.com

FRANÇOIS RABELAIS

FRENCH HUMANIST WRITER

- **Born in Chinon (France) in around 1494.**
- **Died in Paris in 1553.**
- **Notable works:**
  - *Pantagruel* (1532), novel
  - *Gargantua* (1534), novel
  - *Le Tiers Livre* ("The Third Book", 1546), novel

François Rabelais was born in around 1494. He was the son of a lawyer, but decided to take holy orders in around 1510. Men of letters, both monks and laymen, shared their passion for Antiquity and humanism with him. Rabelais left the clergy in 1527 for unknown reasons and went to study medicine at the University of Montpellier. He then moved to Lyon, where he wrote humorous pamphlets and began to correspond with Erasmus (Dutch humanist, 1469-1536). He also published his first two books (*Pantagruel* and *Gargantua*), which were censored by the College of Sorbonne. Rabelais then became the secretary of Jean du Bellay (French bishop and diplomat, 1492/98-1560), who he accompanied to Rome. From 1546, he began to publish sequels to his books, a decision which caused him a lot of trouble with the College of Sorbonne. Some time later, the cardinal managed to get him the position of curate of Meudon, which he resigned from in 1553.

Rabelais was a unique, cultivated and jovial man. He died in 1553 in Paris.

GARGANTUA

FROM GIANT TO GARGANTUAN

- **Genre**: novel
- **Reference edition**: Rabelais, F. (1894) *Gargantua*. Trans. Urquhart, T. Nottingham: Printed and Published for Private Circulation.
- **1st edition**: 1534
- **Themes**: folklore, laughter, parody, education, war, gigantism

Gargantua was published in 1534 in Lyon by François Juste, under the pseudonym Alcofribas Nasier (an anagram of the author's real name, François Rabelais). His first novel, *Pantagruel*, published in 1532, had already been very successful. However, instead of merely continuing the story, Rabelais decided to narrate the life of Pantagruel's father, Gargantua.

The tale was reworked several times and, before its final republication in 1542, the author prudently adjusted several parts of the book which had come under fire. The most notable of these adjustments was changing the words "theologians" and "Sorbonne" to "sophist".

Although the book is the most structured of Rabelais' stories, it still stands out due to its unique, creative use of language. Rabelais is a sceptical, mocking writer and always defends his ideas with the greatest weapon there is: laughter.

SUMMARY

CHILDHOOD AND EDUCATION (CHAPTERS 1-14)

Grangousier the giant marries Gargamelle. She falls pregnant and carries the baby for 11 months, which, according to the narrator, is a sign that the baby will be perfect. Gargamelle goes to a Mardi Gras banquet. In spite of her husband's disapproval, she stuffs herself with tripe, drinks a large amount of wine and dances a lot. It is at this point that she begins to have contractions and gives birth in a rather unusual manner: the child comes out of her ear, shouting "some drink, some drink, some drink." His father, King Grangousier, calls him Gargantua. Feeding the enormous newborn requires thousands of cows.

The child is completely free to do whatever he wants: he drinks, eats, sleeps, chases butterflies, rolls around in the dirt, and so on. His vocabulary is limited to childish gibberish and scatological fables. One day, Gargantua invents the wipebreech. Realising that his son is very intelligent, Grangousier decides to hire him a private tutor by the name of Tubal Holofernes. However, the kind of archaic and sophistic education the man gives him actually makes Gargantua less intelligent. One day Eudemon, an educated page who makes Gargantua look like a fool, shows up. Grangousier realises his mistake and sends his son to study in Paris. He receives an enormous mare as a gift from the King of Numidia, and she becomes Gargantua's steed.

On the road, Gargantua's horse accidently destroys a forest with her tail. When he reaches the capital, Gargantua urinates and drowns the majority of the inhabitants. He then tears out the bells from Our Lady's Church to hang them from the neck of his horse. The survivors send a man called Janotus de Bragmardo to negotiate with him. However, he speaks in such an absurd way that Gargantua finds him comical. Janotus goes to the masters of the College of Sorbonne to be paid, but they refuse. The man immediately brings a suit in law against them. The bells are finally returned, and the Parisians take care of the giant's horse.

Gargantua finally joins his new professor, Ponocrates. The first thing his new master makes him do is drink a potion which wipes his old lessons from his memory. Under the guidance of his experienced teacher, Gargantua begins to develop his critical mind, studies great texts and learns how to use weapons, to list but a few aspects of his education. From time to time, Gargantua leaves the city to unwind and hunt with his esquire Gymnast.

WAR AND TRIUMPH (CHAPTERS 15-44)

In the meantime, there is an altercation in Gargantua's homeland. Some cake-bakers pass by a group of shepherds who are watching over Grangousier's vines. The shepherds ask them for some cakes, but the bakers insult them. Forgier, one of the shepherds, takes offense and begins to lecture them. One of the bakers, Marquet, tells him to come help himself, and then whips him. The shepherd shouts as loud as he can and throws his cudgel at Marquet's head. In the end, the shepherds buy some cakes and settle down to feast.

However, the cake-bakers go to complain to Picrochole, the neighbouring king, who sees an opportunity to declare war on Grangousier. His army ravages the giant's countryside, and the Abbey of Seville is attacked. At this point, Friar John of the funnels and gobbets appears. Alone, he valiantly defends the monastery and temporarily halts Picrochole's troops while the other monks pray.

Grangousier wishes to parley, but Picrochole will not back down. The giant sends a letter to his son, telling him that he has tried everything he can to keep the peace. After the failure of his ambassador, Ulric Gallet, Grangousier decides to pay the cake-sellers and resolve the situation which caused all of this. Picrochole sees this as an admission of weakness and renews hostilities with increased vigour.

Gymnast, sent on a scouting mission by Gargantua, is caught unawares by looters. In order to escape from them, he pretends to be possessed by the devil and begins do all sorts of acrobatics on his horse. After winning a battle at the castle at the ford of Vede, Gargantua goes to meet his father. In order to celebrate his return, a feast is organised. Gargantua almost gobbles up a group of pilgrims who were hiding under some lettuce in the garden. Friar John becomes the young giant's best friend.

The battles continue without respite. Finally, the giants and their friends emerge victorious. Picrochole flees and, in a rage, kills his horse. He tries to steal a donkey, but he is mugged by some millers. Nobody knows what then becomes of him. Gargantua frees the majority of the prisoners, treats all the casualties and lectures the vanquished on the absurdity of this kind of conflict.

THE ABBEY OF THELEME (CHAPTERS 50-58)

As a reward for Friar John's bravery, Gargantua builds him the Abbey of Theleme, the motto of which becomes "Do What Thou Wilt." Its members live in perfect harmony and freedom.

While digging the building's foundations, a mysterious text is discovered. The prophetic puzzle leads to contradictory interpretations, which is where the novel ends.

CHARACTER STUDY

GARGANTUA

Gargantua is the main character of the story. The etymology of his name is clearly linked to the throat: when he was born, Gargantua immediately cried for alcohol, which is why Grangousier exclaimed "How great and nimble a throat thou hast." He is a giant.

Gargantua and his father, Grangousier, are the perfect representations of merciful, protective monarchs:

- they do everything they can to keep the peace in their kingdom;
- they harbour no desire for vengeance;
- after winning the final battle, they refuse to annex the lands that they have conquered, thereby sparing their enemies further humiliation;
- they do not have Picrochole executed, but strip him of his royal privileges, making him no more than an ordinary man.

Many people see Gargantua as an allegory of Francis I, the King of France from 1515-1547, who Rabelais considered the ideal monarch, gifted with an exceptional sense of morality.

THE TUTORS

Holofernes and Bride

Grangousier sends his son to his first tutor, Tubal Holofernes, and then to his second, Jobelin Bride. Gargantua's education (Chapters 8 and 20):

- is governed by his bodily needs (greed, excretion, coughing, and so on) which, in addition, are unpredictable (Gargantua has absolutely no sense of personal hygiene);
- is outdated (it is made up of random elements from the late Middle Ages, purely bookish knowledge and a mixture of works by legal experts and obscure grammarians);
- takes an extremely long time, since it lasts 54 years;
- is based on automatic memory and rote learning: the student does nothing more than mechanically recite texts, forwards and backwards;
- makes him very passive: the tutor just makes him read books, without asking for his participation or input, which leads to the loss of his critical mind and his ability to reflect;
- has no relation with real life.

EUDEMON

Eudemon is the one who highlights how useless the education Gargantua receives from Holofernes and Bride is. The young page is completely different from Gargantua's tutors. He is described as "so neat, so trim [...] and so sweet and comely in his behaviour" (Chapter 15), which gives us a clue as to the efficacy of the education he has received, all the more so when compared to the young giant's schooling, as his former tutors clearly omitted to teach him good manners. Gargantua realises this himself, and begins to cry, ashamed, "hiding it [his face] with his cap", after hearing the talented speech which Eudemon delivers. The young page is therefore the driving element and the turning point of Gargantua's education, because it is at this point that he and his father realise the limits of and the gaps in the education teachers like Holofernes or Bride provide. After this, Grangousier wishes to entrust his child's education to Eudemon's tutor, Ponocrates.

PONOCRATES

Ponocrates offers Gargantua a new style of education based on:

- **Humanist knowledge**. His teaching is based on classical Greek and Latin authors, as well as other humanist works such as *In Praise of Folly* (1511) by Erasmus and *Utopia* (1515-1516) by Thomas More (1478-1535). Ponocrates also opens Gargantua's eyes to the sciences which were developing at the time (astronomy, biology, mathematics, medicine). Finally, a lot of importance is accorded to the interpretation of religious texts: the pupil's day begins and ends with an examination of the Bible, so that he will learn to understand it better.
- **Discipline of the body and the organisation of time**. The harmony between the body and spirit is re-established (*Mens sana in corpore sano*, "a healthy mind in a healthy body"): Gargantua learns to wash himself, do

physical exercise, and so on. He also learns to manage his time in a different way. He gets up before dawn and no longer wastes a moment of the day. Each waking hour is associated with an activity and there is no room for idleness. Moreover, several things are done at the same time: he learns while he is getting dressed, while he is washing, while he is eating, and so on. However, keeping up this pace must be exhausting, which is why Rabelais does not demand that the complete programme be followed to the letter. It is rather an ideal which indicates the overall perspective of the learning that he advises.

- **A range of learning methods**. When the intellectual tension becomes overwhelming, outdoor conversations, games and physical, military-style exercises are used as an outlet.
- **The student's reflection**. This is a time for Gargantua to develop his critical mind and learn to think for himself.
- **Practical sense**. Rabelais' programme is not cut off from reality; it does not neglect practical life. Knowledge is acquired hand in hand with the study of nature and society: direct observation and experimentation complete Gargantua's education. Moreover, Gargantua also studies the sciences, geography and even astronomy, fields which were neglected by his previous tutors.

HUMANISM

In Western history, humanism is a school of thought which first appeared in Italy in the 14th century and then spread throughout Europe in the 15th and 16th centuries. It is characterised by a return to Antiquity and a limitless faith in man's moral and intellectual capacities. For humanists, the thirst for knowledge and the development of critical thinking elevates humans, allowing us to improve ourselves and understand Creation. Teaching is therefore at the centre of this school of thought. The rediscovery of texts from Antiquity, the foundations of humanism, was seen as a true renaissance and allowed the birth of modern sciences. Rabelais was one of the great humanists of the 16th century.

Through Holofernes and Bride, Rabelais makes a mockery of traditional scholastic education. This teaching, which began to be developed in the 11th century and reached its peak in the 13th century, aimed to unite Christian belief with reason. It taught students bookish knowledge which had no relationship to real life and required no reflection, comprehension or intelligence. Rabelais considers this way of teaching too rigid, mind-numbing and unsuitable for the times. Gargantua comes away ignorant, wordy and pretentious. Grangousier realises the extent of his error when Eudemon (from Greek, meaning "the happy one" or "the fortunate one"), a young page educated according to humanist principles, shows up. The contrast with his son is so obvious that the king decides to find him a tutor like Eudemon's, and comes across Ponocrates (from Greek, meaning "he who withstands effort"). The openness and completeness of humanist education makes Gargantua into a person who deserves to be listened to. From now on, the protagonist is capable of thinking for himself and is versed in Greek, Latin and Erasmian knowledge. His education validates his position in society: through speech, Gargantua is capable of influencing and guiding men's actions. As a result, Rabelais uses Gargantua to highlight and praise humanist education.

GYMNAST

Gymnast does not appear until Chapter 23, while Gargantua is being taught by Ponocrates. While Ponocrates takes care of Gargantua's intellectual development, Gymnast teaches him chivalry. He is like a complementary twin of the model character of Eudemon. While Eudemon stands out mostly due to the subtlety and the quality of his speech, Gymnast, a real master of acrobatics, displays the full extent of his talents in the battles with Picrochole's forces, during which he crushes his enemies with considerable skill. Gymnast, whose name means "the agile one", can be seen as the perfect example of physical perfection, a perfection which he tries to help Gargantua attain. As we have seen elsewhere in the book, this is a way of praising humanist education, as there is an equal balance between caring for one's body and searching for knowledge. What is more, Gymnast is not just a brawler; he shows wisdom too, such as when he defeats Captain Tripet ("it becomes all cavaliers modestly to use their good fortune, without troubling or stretching it too far"), just like Eudemon, who is the paradigm of well-rounded knowledge, since he already has beautiful physical features.

PICROCHOLE

Picrochole, the King of Lerne, is impulsive and aggressive. His name means "the bad-tempered one." He declares war over a simple village quarrel. He embodies the furious conqueror who forgets peace treaties and is obsessed with himself.

If Gargantua is Francis I, Picrochole is his rival Charles V (Holy Roman Emperor, 1500-1558). When he came to power, he ruled over a territory which included Spain and its colonies, the Kingdom of the Two Sicilies (Naples), Burgundy and the Seventeen Provinces. In 1519, he was elected Holy Roman Emperor. With his European territories and his Spanish colonies, he literally inherited an empire "on which the sun never sets." His motto, *"Plus ultra"* can be translated as "further beyond", and implies that there were no more boundaries to territorial expansion.

For Rabelais, the episode of the war with Picrochole is an opportunity to denounce the excesses of war. Like all humanists, he advocates peace and diplomacy. Grangousier, the embodiment of the ideal monarch in Rabelais' eyes, opts for the diplomatic approach. Since he is a kindly ruler, his principal concern is the repercussions of a war for his subjects, and he tries to appease his adversary by whatever means necessary. But Grangousier's best efforts fall short, as Picrochole refuses to see reason. Faced with such an insurmountable obstacle, the giants resign themselves to war, regretfully, but without showing the slightest weakness: they elaborate a firm, methodical strategy.

FRIAR JOHN OF THE FUNNELS AND GOBBETS

Friar John may be ignorant, but he is also a pragmatic, daring monk who cares about the problems of his time. Meeting him gives the hero the chance to contest the usefulness of monks and prayer. When Friar John becomes Gargantua's friend, the two form a duo which calls to mind that of Pantagruel and Panurge. In both cases, the distinguished hero is accompanied by a less educated antihero. The interpretation of events always sways between the vision of one of the two, which is often allegorical, and that of the other, which is very prosaic. We see this with the final puzzle, when Gargantua believes he is reading a symbolic text while Friar John sees nothing more than a description of *jeu de paume*.

ANALYSIS

A MIXED WORK: FROM A FAIRGROUND CHARACTER TO A CIVILISING HERO

In order to write *Gargantua*, Rabelais drew inspiration from various sources, including folklore, novels, chivalric romances and humanism.

Gargantua was originally a popular folkloric character from traditional oral stories. An anonymous transcription of his adventures was written in 1532: *Grandes et Inestimables Chroniques du grand et énorme géant Gargantua* ("The Great and Inestimable Chronicles of the Great and Enormous Giant Gargantua"), which featured a great deal of bawdy jokes and sometimes even obscenity. This carnivalesque tale recounts the life of a naïve giant in the service of King Artus, and was a very popular fairground story. Rabelais only kept some scenes from the original tale, such as the theft of the bells of Our Lady's Church.

The primitive 1532 story had already linked Gargantua to the Arthurian tales of legend. However, Rabelais also based his story on chivalric romances. After introducing the protagonist's fabulous, mythical heritage, he describes other episodes which are typically found in this genre: the miraculous birth of the hero, the revelation of his potential, his education, his exploration of the world, the exploits which prove his valour, his battles and his eventual triumph.

The influence of other genres, including poems, conversations and lectures, can also be found in the tale.

Finally, by adding the considerations of humanist men of letters (such as education, the wars with Picrochole, the utopia of Theleme, and so on) to the story, Rabelais makes the main character into a civilising hero.

This mixture of genres came as a surprise to 17th-century readers. Rabelais forces extremes to coexist within a paradoxical universe. However, it should be noted that this liberty taken by the writer does not prevent his novel from making sense, quite the contrary.

THE PROMOTION OF HUMANIST IDEAS AND A CRITIQUE OF THE MEDIEVAL INTELLECTUAL TRADITION

Rabelais' novel is completely in sync with his time and develops and explores the great questions which animated society in those days. The humanist branch of philosophy goes completely against the scholastic tradition of the Middle Ages, which was seen as paralysing, and Rabelais makes an important contribution to it with the original methods of farce and parody. The comic effect is most striking when the incoherent buffoons of sophistry are described, or when the excesses of the scholars of the College of Sorbonne are brought up. We see how the balance of the humanist principles is far superior to the absurdities of scholastic education. Scrupulous hygiene and respect for one's body on one side, sloppiness on the other (theologians sometimes considered looking after the body as a sign of according too much attention to the material, and therefore a sin); a return to the direct study of biblical texts against strictly formalist and quantitative religious practice; physical exercises versus gluttony and excessive drinking... The pitiful results obtained with the first tutors highlight the amount of time which is lost with this kind of education. Gargantua spends the majority of his time at banquets and in ritualised prayers instead of learning and developing himself seriously. Humanist education, on the other hand, attempts to develop knowledge by focusing on reflection and critical thinking, without forgetting the essential maintenance of the physical faculties which are necessary for good health.

We witness the development of a real programme rather than just a comparison between two different ways of doing things, a programme which makes searching for the right balance the core of all healthy progression. It is important to find balance between intellectual knowledge, moral reflexion and physical upkeep, between work and rest, between art and science, and between theoretical knowledge and practical experience. And, above all, the author sets out a very novel idea for the time: the importance of the active participation of the student himself during his education, during which he is invited to constantly reflect and ask himself questions. However, Rabelais never lets himself be caught up in one programme, and rightly so: the winds of freedom and gigantism which blow through these pages, dedicated to themes that were of vital importance to the intellectual and philosophical adventures of his time, remain the guiding force of the novel. Comedy, which serves as a powerful weapon against the shortcomings of the educational traditions of his time, also inspires more free and colourful literary creation.

MEANING BEHIND THE LAUGHTER

The preface addresses us directly and suggests a particular kind of reading: we should chew the bones and "suck out the marrow". Rabelais invites his readers to not be satisfied with the literal meaning of the book; we need to go further than that. In other words, we should not take the book at face value. The author wants us to gradually read between the lines. *Gargantua* is therefore far from simply being an amusing tale.

Indeed, the comic vividness is only pointless at first glance. Between the burlesque, ridiculous episodes we can find more subtle elements. If an informed reader dissects certain passages, they will discover a multitude of references to the problems of their time, whether they are philosophical, moral or religious. Some of the most notable themes Rabelais touches upon include war, which he criticises, the qualities of a good monarch, and the characteristics of a good education.

Rabelais' tale therefore encourages debate, puzzles and discursive questioning, albeit in a rather jovial and grotesque tone. No single, unambiguous reading can fix the meaning of the tale. Reading is a pretext to reflect on the world: it invites us to reflect, stirs up debate and allows us to form our own judgements. The reader is therefore involved in the reading process.

RABELAIS' SENSE OF COMEDY

Rabelais' tale is extremely comic. Melancholy has no place in this book: all the stories unfold with enthusiasm. Indeed, the principal aim of the author is to make his reader laugh. In his opinion, laughter has a healing quality: it relieves anxiety, fatigue, melancholy, and other ailments. As a doctor, Rabelais wrote his novels primarily to cure his patients. He uses several techniques to do this: gigantism, verbal invention, parody and exaggeration.

Gigantism

Giants, which are really no more than enlarged humans, are present in all sorts of folklore. They are a source of comedy thanks to the simple contrast with our average humanity: we therefore laugh at the description of Gargantua's build, at the amount of material needed to clothe him and at all the objects which have been made specifically for him. It should also be noted that gigantism allows the author to be very audacious and very critical, while still protecting the modesty of the public and of contemporary society.

Verbal invention

Rabelais astonishes and makes us laugh with his language. He mixes technical terms, onomatopoeias and ancient, strange, and dialectal words. He is also the father of many neologisms in the French language – such as "ramentevoir" ("bethink"), "pamparigouste" ("Timbuktu"), "coquecigrue"("chimera"), "croquelardon" ("scrounger"), "goguelu" ("vainglorious"), "matagraboliser" ("matagrabolising"), "trepelu" ("Touquedillon") – and proverbs which have now become classic, including:

- "to laugh is proper to the man" (Prologue)
- "it is not the habit makes the monk" (Prologue)
- "appetite comes with eating" (Chapter 5).

Moreover, his sentences are sprinkled with wordplay, puns and spoonerisms: "The great God made the planets, and we make the platters neat" (ibid.).

Parody

Rabelais makes frequent use of parody, breaking the existing norms. He therefore mixes noble subjects and trivial topics, which leads to comical situations.

He notably parodies the chivalric code, which he considers to be obsolete and unrealistic (Chapter 34). When faced with the blind, stupid strength of their adversaries, the giants and their friends prefer to fight back with wits and humour.

In tales of knights:

- the protagonists use noble weapons (swords, lances);
- the enemies are disciplined, upstanding men who are vanquished in combat in an honourable fashion;
- the warriors resist blows without being slowed by their injuries.

Instead, here:

- Gargantua uses an uprooted tree while his enemies use firearms;
- the enemies are cowards (deserters and looters) and they die in ridiculous ways (drowned in the giant mare's urine);
- Gargantua mistakes cannonballs for grape seeds and flies.

Exaggeration

Rabelais' characters take a great deal of pleasure in extraordinary lists, exact numbers, useless details, fantastic hyperbole, improper comparisons, the repetition of words and expressions, and so on.

For example, Picrochole's advisers know to pander to his megalomaniac pride (Chapter 31). Encouraging his imperialistic frenzy, they envisage conquering the entire world. In order to ensure their speech will please him, they take Alexander the Great (King of Macedon, 356-323 BC) as a model and make a long list of conquered regions, even going so far as to make up the names of countries. Moreover, these inventions repeat the same sounds, which creates the impression of a nursery rhyme. In order to make themselves seem more credible, they also mention excessively precise numbers. It is not as issue if their suggestions are foolish.

UTOPIA: THE ABBEY OF THELEME

At the end of the story, Friar John is rewarded for his bravery with the Abbey of Theleme, which becomes the seat of a new kind of religious organisation. The abbey is the cradle of a perfect new society, made up of beautiful, rich, cultured and educated young people. Life there entails neither conflict nor disagreement.

By describing what the inhabitants do there, Rabelais highlights what they do not do. As a result, he takes the complete opposite stance of the extremely restrictive monastic rules which he personally lived through. Indeed, Theleme is a place of diversity and freedom of speech and movement. Everyone is free to say and do as they please: in Greek, *thelema* means "free will." In addition, all vows of chastity, poverty and obedience are abolished.

The monastery's motto is "Do What Thou Wilt." However, if everyone only does what they want, there cannot be a genuine community: how can mutual respect and moral elevation be assured? How can excess and licentiousness be fought? In fact, Rabelais supposes that exercising individual freedom encourages the pursuit of the common good. The abbey's system therefore corresponds to the confidence that Rabelais, just like all humanists of his time, places in human nature.

The utopia of Theleme is a symbol more than a real project. Indeed, this ideal place is too harmonious, too well-run and, above all, is not made for the giants and their friends. Rabelais' characters are beings of dialogue. They feel the need to travel a world which is constantly moving and changing, the source of tireless controversies and malicious scandals. In Theleme, the need for unity crushes all difference. Every word is drowned in the collective will. The author therefore cannot keep his creatures there, because that would be the same as keeping them prisoner. It would erase their differences, which are so charming and laden with meaning. Moreover, the Abbey of Theleme will be quickly forgotten in the books which follow. Nothing can curb man's desire to question the world.

RECEPTION OF THE NOVEL

As with all of Rabelais' novels, *Gargantua*'s success varies with its readers and the times. Although *Pantagruel* did not raise the suspicions of the censors and was simply criticised for its obscenity, everything changed with the release of *Gargantua*. In a context of growing religious persecution, texts and their "marrow" became suspicious, which explains why Rabelais had few open admirers of his work in his time, despite the widespread distribution of the book.

With the passing of time and the author's comments which made him out to be a buffoonish, alcoholic writer, Rabelais always managed to stir up strong reactions, a fact which speaks volumes about the power of his novel. His fight against obscurantism and for individual freedom, as well as his subversive, creative use of language and the novel form, continue to be discussed and inspire others in French literature, from moralists to the most modern authors, including Romantics and the thinkers of the Enlightenment.

FURTHER REFLECTION

SOME QUESTIONS TO THINK ABOUT...

- What differences can we see between Rabelais' giants and, for example, fairy-tale ogres?
- How do the characters' names reveal their character? Explain using examples from the book.
- In Chapter 5, what techniques does Rabelais use to make us believe that the events he is recounting are true? What details make the reader realise that Rabelais is actually not being serious?
- Find the text of the *Rule of Saint Benedict* (written for Benedictine monks around 540) and compare its content with the system of the Abbey of Theleme. What do you notice?
- Friar John's interpretation of the world opposes that of Gargantua. How does this difference in views come back to the image of a bone to chew and of the soft marrow within?
- Behind the comedy lie far more serious topics. Explain what Rabelais' version of comedy is and what his more serious objectives are.
- Rabelais urges us to go beyond the literal reading of the novel. By extension, he would no doubt suggest the same approach with religious texts (with the Bible, for example). Explain this statement.
- "In *Gargantua*, there is a certain ambiguity which hangs throughout the novel." Justify this theory.
- In your opinion, are there any similarities between *Gargantua* and *Don Quixote* by Cervantes (published

between 1605 and 1615)?

- Erasmus' *In Praise of Folly* uses satire as a weapon in intellectual combat. In what way is this similar to what Rabelais does in *Gargantua*?
- What makes Rabelais a humanist?
- What distinctions can you make between the duo of Gargantua and Pantagruel and the group formed in *Le Tiers Livre* ("The Third Book"), *Le Quart Livre* ("The Fourth Book") et *Le Cinquième Livre* ("The Fifth Book")?

We want to hear from you!
Leave a comment on your online library
and share your favourite books on social media!

FURTHER READING

REFERENCE EDITION

- Rabelais, F. (1894) *Gargantua*. Trans. Urquhart, T. Nottingham: Printed and Published for Private Circulation.

REFERENCE STUDIES

- Merritt, Y. (No date) The Unquenchable Thirst to Understand: Francois Rabelais' Satire of Medieval and Renaissance Learning In 'Gargantua and Pantagruel'. *Ampersand: the science of art; the art of science.* [Online]. Volume 2. [Accessed 3 April 2017]. Available from: <http://itech.fgcu.edu/&/issues/vol2/issue2/rabelais.htm>
- Gioia, T. (No date) 'Gargantua and Pantagruel' by François Rabelais. *Conceptual Fiction.* [Online]. [Accessed 3 April 2017]. Available from: <http://www.conceptualfiction.com/Gargantua_and_Pantagruel.html>

MORE FROM BRIGHTSUMMARIES.COM

- Reading guide – *Pantagruel* by François Rabelais.

www.brightsummaries.com

Ebook EAN: 9782806296542

Paperback EAN: 9782806296559

Legal Deposit: D/2017/12603/219

This guide was written with the collaboration of Marc Sigala for the sections 'Eudemon' and 'Gymnast' and the chapters 'The promotion of humanist ideas and a critique of the medieval intellectual tradition' and 'Reception of the novel'.

Cover: © Primento

Digital conception by Primento, the digital partner of publishers.

Printed in Great Britain
by Amazon